WtF

I'M 50 AND

GAY

S.D. DOGAN

The most difficult part about anyone's life is acceptance. Acceptance of self is critical. I always believed that I knew myself wholeheartedly, with all my flaws, fears and, imperfections. I found out after a century of living that life changes, we adapt, and those feelings I experienced at twelve should have been enough, but fear, doubt, and society made me choose a life that should never have been mine. Now it's time for me to create new memories with my wife in tow, and the great part about experiences is finding them in obscure places.

Experience this journey with me as I explore my sexuality, revisit my memories, and welcome a renewed self-discovery that stems from being a part of the LBGT community. This book is dedicated to those family members and friends (you know who you are) who encouraged me to walk in my truth with pride and confidence and live my life unapologetically as a bi-sexual woman. I will cherish and love you forever.

tHe FIRSt tiMe

One afternoon, my best friend and I decided to hang out. "Hanging out" to a twelve-year-old meant being holed up in your room, playing dress up, borrowing your mother's lipstick, and acting grown up. This time I sensed something was different about Shawn. She applied her mother's red lipstick to her lips, walked across the room with her high heels on as if she had worn them a million times before, and posed. She turned around to look at me with a wicked grin. She was up to something. "Let's play house," she said. House? I hadn't played house since I was five. Why they hell would we play house now? "You can be the daddy," she told me. Walking back toward me, she stopped. "We will play house and you will pretend you just came home from work, and I will greet you." "Okay," I said, standing up to face her. She continued to walk toward me. In heels her four-foot frame seemed six feet tall. She was thin, bony really, but she always had boobs and a butt. And for the first time, I was checking her out. She smiled. Could she tell I was staring? I wasn't quite sure. "Okay," she said "You're the daddy, and I have to greet you when you come home. You stay there, and I will come to you." I stood frozen in place as she approached me. She appeared to slither over toward me snake-like. Standing in front

1

of me, she looked down and said, "Welcome home daddy." She leaned in and kissed me. I was shocked by the contact of her lips on mine. No one girl or boy had ever kissed me before. I froze. She leaned back and asked if I was happy to see her. I could only nod yes. She leaned in again, and this time I returned the kiss and even let her tongue touch mine. She walked away and told me that daddies get rewards for working hard all day. Did I want my reward? Even my twelve-year-old horny self knew I wanted a reward. Yes, I nodded my head up and down. I was told to lie down on the floor for the reward, so I did as I was told. She pulled up my skirt (yes, even play daddies get forced to wear skirts) and touched my privates, asking me if I liked my reward. Well, I wasn't sure what the reward was supposed to be, so I told her I didn't like the reward. So, she slid my panties to the side and fingered me. My body responded and I became wet. I liked this game of mommy and daddy. She told me that mommies check on daddies and licked my wetness. We played this game every Wednesday for the remainder of the summer, until she moved with her aunt down south.

After my first experience with a girl, I wanted more, but I was afraid to seek out girls from my school, or neighborhood for that matter. I saw girls dressed like boys all the time but wasn't interested in how they looked. I liked those girls who wore jeans but not boots and baseball shirts. It had been a while since I had had my first experience at twelve. Now at seventeen and in high school, I wanted another opportunity before I had to start dating guys like all my friends. Hiding my desire was getting harder than I thought. I had to learn to keep my head down when I walked the halls of the school, as I had begun to stare when girls walked by. Nowadays, staring made them think I wanted to fight, but all I wanted to do was touch their asses. I don't know why I was so fixated on women's butts. Probably because I didn't have one of my own, lol. Then one day, I saw her walking the halls with her friends. She was loud, cracking jokes on the guys as she walked by. I leaned up against the locker and watched the action as she walked past me. Our eyes connected for a split second, and I thought she was cute enough to look at, but did I want her to be my second encounter? I wasn't certain she was interested in girls. I observed from a distance for a while, then started following her daily routine, I began to stalk her. One day, I leaned against my locker and watched her walk by, but this time she stared hard at me instead of giving me the quick glance from the prior days. She walked away from her friends and came over to my side of the hall and asked me if I was okay. I didn't expect that question, but I told her I was fine. She wanted to know why I was staring at her. I told her to meet me after school near the basketball courts if she wanted to know. Damn, I was ballsy. At exactly 3 p.m. she met me at the court with her friends in tow. Why the hell did she have her friends with her? I stood alone and she approached me. "Are you going to tell me why you were staring?" she said. I was hoping you would come by yourself, why the crowd? I wanted to know. They wanted to know if you would stop staring and join the club. The club? What club, I thought to myself. I was so clueless when it came to life. The girls and she belonged to a club where they hung out at each other's houses and had fun. What kind of fun, I wanted to know. "We have sexual encounters with each other," she said. I thought they all had boyfriends, I told her. As I stood under the evening sky, she began to run it down for me. They all had "friends" that were boys that they hung out with at school, only never at home, because they didn't want people to think they were dykes (this was the term used in the '80s). At home and on the weekends, they hung out with each other, and whoever wanted to try something could—there were no rules. Since there was only three of them, it was good to have another person join them, and maybe they would pair off more. I wasn't interested in having any kind of intimacy with several girls. I only liked her, so I told her that. I was offered a trial "date." I could come to her house over the weekend and spend the night, so that she could test out whether I could join their group. Shoot, it was only Wednesday; Saturday would take forever.

I had to find a way to stay busy until Saturday morning. I spent some time studying—more than I normally did. Ran errands for my mother and aunt to the grocery store several times through the days leading up to Saturday. Mostly I just watched the clock; days ticked down to hours, then minutes, and finally Saturday arrived, and I was up early, pacing the floor with the anticipation of what the day would bring, waiting on her to call so I could head over to her house. The sun was beginning to set, when around 4 p.m. my house phone rang. It was her. Hanging up the phone, I was sprinting down the block and around the corner before she had a chance to even say goodbye. I ran all the way to her house, not giving any thought to the sweat rolling down my chest. Arriving at her door, I was ushered into the living room, where I discovered that her mother had left for work and was not coming back until Sunday at noon. Apparently, this was the norm at her house. We made our way to her room, which was in the back of the house—the room farthest away from her mother's bedroom. Once inside, she informed me that to be a part of the group, I needed to be skilled in orgasms, both giving them and receiving them. Remembering that I only wanted her and not the group, I managed to muster up enough courage to tell her that the only person I wanted to give an orgasm to was her. I thought that I would change her mind later and was convinced I watched enough porno movies to be able to pull her, and I was desperate to try. Laying her down on her bed, there was no need to talk about what was going to happen—now was the time for action. I removed every stitch of her clothing because I truly wanted to admire her body. Hovering above her, I just looked into her eyes, remembering that time at twelve years old when I was asked if I was ready. Instead of asking for permission, I dove in headfirst . . . I was home!

tHeRe SHe WAS . . .

I was no longer seventeen. The years had been good to me—same cute face but with more maturity and intelligence than ever before. I had tucked away those desires of my youth until thirty years later, when she walked into my office, short and thick. So thick, I thought her ass was talking to me. There seemed to be no separation between her ass and thighs. Cute face, stud like, and I got lost in her cat-like light brown eyes. She was happy I had returned to our hometown, and by happenstance, I was hired at her firm. She made it a point to stop by my office to say hello to me daily. Always slightly flirting, but never asking me outright if I was still interested in women. I pretended not to notice her subtle flirtatious ways. Besides, she came on to everyone all day long. Why was I different? Why did I want to be different? I had a man at home that was kind, generous, and semi-supportive, but lacking in areas that I needed. Intimacy was nonexistent and the sex was whack. Did I just say whack? Well yes, it was boring as hell. He was a selfish lover, and I rarely ever had an orgasm. Orgasms only occurred when I sat on his face, which wasn't that often. I was tired and bored and was searching for some excitement. I had been married twice before, and each time, I was left wanting more of something, but I was never sure of what that something was. In those relationships, the spark did not stay lit, there were no meaningful conversations, growth potential, or similar interest. I was married in name only but lived my own life, searching for that missing piece. And she stood there, looking at me with those eyes. Some slick shit came out of her mouth, "it's been a while I'm not a kid anymore; you should try the adult version." I wasn't interested in changing anything about my life, but my normal daily response of "go ahead with that" did not seem to fit the occasion this time. So instead, I told her, "Oh trust me, I want to try it." She froze—I don't think she ever thought I would respond that way. She laughed it off and left, more like ran off; my story, my version, lol.

We played this cat-and-mouse game for a few weeks longer. She would come into my office, flirt, and leave. Her comments were getting bolder every day. One day, she came in and reported that her coworkers were beginning to talk about her frequent morning visits. Rumors were spreading about a relationship between the two of us that was nonexistent. She decided to stop visiting to protect my reputation. Unknown to me, she had a long time off-again on-again relationship with one of her coworkers, but we will get to that story later. She intentionally stayed away from me, believing that the rumors would die down. She hoped that in time I would come around to her advances, but she didn't want anyone to know that she was equally as interested. She knew I was intrigued, but what she did not know was how much. I waited patiently to get a glimpse of her. Three days passed without a word.

Bi-sexual since twelve, I knew what sex with a woman was like, and I yearned for her to be my first adult experience, since she had turned me out as a kid. Sitting in my office and pretending to work, I heard her voice. Today was the day, or so I thought, that I would tell her that I wanted her. I saw her walking through the lobby, and our eyes connected. Focusing on nothing and no one else, I walked across the lobby area, not stopping for those who called my name. My mind was set on the prize standing near the window. I wanted her. I approached eagerly, needing to be close to her. Standing in front of her, I just looked into her eyes. "Ms. T you weren't visiting me today?" I said. She turned and checked me out from head to toe. Her response, "Gotcha!"

She was playing a game. Why do we humans do that to each other? There always seems to have to be someone in charge. Who's holding the title of the leader of the relationship. Its always better when you have shared understanding, values, and equal respect for one another. I was fifty and gay and didn't have time for childish games. I had played them all throughout my failed marriages, pulling my kids along for my crazy rides in search of myself. I was a grandmother now and wanted someone who was willing to fly off into the sunset with me. Sharing equally in our wins and losses. Was she the one because I wanted her to be, or because I needed her to be? I wrestled with these thoughts for weeks after her "gotcha" comment. I wasn't quite dug into the relationship yet. My feet hadn't returned to the pond, per se. Internally, I was struggling, I had managed to keep my sexuality a secret my entire life. I had told no one, not even my bestie Bean. Wondering, or more like worrying about, what people would say, how they would perceive me. I was the GOAT in my family. I was the one people called, confided in, and depended on. I knew where all the bones were hidden, mostly because I was there with the shovel. But she was different, and I was tired of hiding. I was able to have real conversations with her that never centered around sex. Sexual physical attraction only lasted so long—I needed meaningful, stimulating conversations. I wanted a best-friend type of situation because I got bored easily. I discovered that she hadn't travelled as much as I had, but she wasn't afraid to fly.

This may seem like a small thing, but for someone who lives for travel and the experience of life, this topic is so important. If she didn't like to travel, she could not be a prospective life partner. So, we tested our potential friendship with each other.

tODAY, We ARe JUSt FRIeNDS.

The Essence Festival is the black folk's pilgrimage. Hundreds of thousands of us congregate in New Orleans during the Fourth of July weekend to connect, party, drink, dance, and have sex. The movie "Girls Trip" had everyone flocking to New Orleans the summer after the movie came out, and I was no different. I even managed to stay at the same hotel where parts of the movie had been filmed. I had been in New Orleans for two days, with my sister and cousins questioning why I had told Ms. T where I would be. Even hooking her up with the same travel agent. I was bragging about going, never expecting her to show up, but she did. I know she was hoping she would get to spend some time with me away from the office, but I was too afraid. Looking out the window, I saw hundreds of people—mostly women—walking down canal street. Me, I was hiding out from her. I went to the gym and worked out much earlier than I said I would be, in order to avoid seeing her. She texted, giving me an update of her whereabouts throughout the day; however, I made sure I was always on the other side of the city. Even if I wasn't, I pretended to be, ducking behind objects as I walked when I thought I saw someone who looked like her. I knew she would not cause a scene in front of my family, but I was not ready to face her. What if I said something so that others could hear? Hiding my true self from others was most important, above everything else. No one in my family or friend circle knew about my desire to be with a woman. I certainly wasn't ready to confess it to the world—I was barely able to confess it to myself. I knew what and who I liked. I knew what moved me emotionally, sexually, and stimulated my senses. But the struggle for acceptance was real. Emotionally, I wasn't ready. Besides, she had not come alone either. She told me she was with a friend, but I later found out it was a "situation." Good thing I stayed away until I was ready. Ready to respond without staring, without that lustful look on my face, without everyone reading my body language. The last two days before we were scheduled to leave, she located me. Damn, she still looked good. I was trapped. My sister immediately bonded with her "situation," so we all hung out together, did a little shopping, and I managed to touch her a few times without anyone noticing. At the Alex and Annie store, I picked out a bracelet with a heart surrounded by two hands. That was the first gift she gave me. I wanted her to know that she had my heart already, even if I didn't communicate it verbally to her.

I love to dance, so we ended up going to a karaoke place where they played line dance music at the end of the night. Line dancing is my favorite, and as I danced in the crowd, I peered up at her looking lustfully down at me. I showed off my moves, gyrating my ass and putting extra bounce in my body for attention. Well, she noticed, and we stared at each other while I continued to dance through the end of the song. While walking back to the hotel, my sister decided she wanted fried chicken. Why is it that we always want something fried and greasy after a night of drinking? Was my sister blocking? I was going to have to walk her to the restaurant. As we made our way to the front door of the hotel, the "situation" offered to walk with her. Whew, I dodged a bullet. I just needed a few minutes alone with Ms. T to talk, since this was our last night in New Orleans.

We headed up to her room in search of a quiet space. She stood against the wall of this extremely small room, with two double beds, looking across the room at me. We began to talk, her on her side and me on mine. Making sure not to move toward each other, we just stared. The room began to shrink, we stood looking at one another and began to discuss our feelings, expectations, commitment, and secrecy. Secrecy was the primary piece of the conversation. We both were involved in other relationships. She was married to a man. Now, normally I would have run the other way. Cheating is a big no-no, but this was magnetic, even electric chemistry. And no matter how much I had tried to fight it over the course of the several months prior to this trip, we kept coming back to each other. Twenty minutes later our friendship was solidified, and that conversation was the beginning of our love story. But it was also the first time she lied to me. Of course I flat-out asked about her "situation". Shockingly, I was told they were just platonic friends who were never intimate with each other. Why are women just like men? Even when they have an out, they still lie. Thinking back on it, I would have lied too. The "situation" was not anything to look at. You know what people say when the person isn't attractive: "she had a great personality." I would have said she was a man in a wig, if I did not know any better. She was subpar in looks but was nice enough to be around. She and my sister were ghetto soul mates—loud, obnoxious, and needy. They connected in New Orleans. While I was busy hiding out, they found each other and were hanging out as long-lost friends. I originally thought she might be trouble. She was not my competition, but I found out the hard way who was.

FIRSt KISS . . .

I used the connections that my sister made in New Orleans with the "situation" to see her again. It was July 23, my sister's birthday. She wanted a little get-together at my house because, of course, she has no friends; well, no friends that would celebrate her birthday for free. As her little big sister (inside joke), it is my job, my responsibility to look out for her. My mind was set on other things, though. I hadn't seen Ms. T since New Orleans, and I was feigning. As much as I wanted to see her, I knew it was wrong to bring her to my home. Who brings their crush to their home when their mate is there? I guess I do. I had to get her outside of the office setting, but I wasn't quite ready for what would happen if we weren't chaperoned. Things were heating up with the conversations, but I had not touched her yet. Tonight was going to be the night. While the ladies stood around the kitchen island drinking red wine and talking crap, she followed me downstairs under the guise of me showing off my finished basement. There was not much to see; just the 20 x 20 patch of burnt grass in the yard, a couple of sofas, and a television in the family room. I was so nervous, I needed a drink. I was fearful of getting caught by my friends and sister in the space above. They had no idea what I wanted to do. I'm sure my sister would never have suggested I show her around if she did. Walking through the small space, I could feel her eyes on me and smell her scent. She smelled of Calvin Klein perfume, and she was aroused; I could tell by her breathing. I tried to take her into the utility area of the basement, but she pulled me into the powder room and placed her soft small lips against my quivering large ones. I devoured her lips immediately, sucking on the bottom one and dueling with her tongue. I was a goner—thirty sections felt like an eternity. I wanted more, so I took her into my arms, holding her so close, our bodies became one. I pushed against her and caressed her back, butt, and perky small boobs. She felt amazing. If we did not have to hide from everyone on the level above, this would have been perfect. But I was straight, or so I kept telling myself in order to make sense of what was swirling around in my head. I needed to find an answer to what I was feeling. These emotions were driving me crazy, and I volleyed between men and women. I'm thinking okay, you like men and I do too, but you like women as well and you have forever. Why do you keep going back to thinking you're straight? I constantly battled with myself inside my head. Tried to focus on what and who was in front of me. WTF! I'm fifty and gay; I hid my entire life behind doing what was "normal." I got married, had kids, and now, as a grandmother, I was holding on to the person who was the most important to me in the entire world. No one knew my secret, and no one ever would. I would do everything to protect my image from the world.

CAUGHt

He crept up the carpeted steps, holding his breath as he went. She had a friend upstairs, someone he knew very well, someone who was known to like women, but who had a husband. Why was she here? he thought to himself, his heart beating faster the closer he got to the top of the stairs. It was quiet in the kitchen as he stood at the door, straining to hear. He pulled the door slowly, so as not the bring attention to himself. He was relieved that the door did not click. He opened the door wide and froze. He could not believe his eyes; they were kissing passionately. His future wife and that woman, holding onto each other lustfully. He lost his voice; the words wouldn't push through. He had so many things he wanted to say. His heart sank. All kinds of thoughts went through his mind. Being shocked was an understatement; he was pissed and disappointed. He had never realized she was into women. She had never mentioned a word to him. How could she do this to him after all he had given to her, he thought. Their entire relationship flashed before his eyes as he tried to recall all the times she had hung out with her girlfriends. Was she seeing one of them as well? After what seemed like an eternity, he slammed the door behind himself. The two women jumped apart from each other, startled by the noise, not real-

17

izing what he had seen, or at least wanting to pretend that he had not seen much. Damn, she said to herself, I just fucked this up. Why did I ask her to come to my house? I should have known better. He knew this trick from work, and she must have been after his future fiancé' for a while now. He had not known they were friends; she always said she only associated with people from her old job. Shit! What was he going to do now? Pretending that he had not witnessed them kissing, he moved away from the door, focusing on the food that awaited him in the oven. He could not draw himself to face either of them. He did not say a word, crying internally and hating everyone in the room. Standing in front of the oven, he heard a voice saying, "What are you cooking for dinner?" WTF! It was her, the dyke; if she was not a woman, he would have smashed her head onto the countertop. Is this dyke crazy? How dare she say anything to me after I just saw her kissing my girl? And my girl seems happy, looking around the room smiling to herself. She better not even look at me. I threw the food on the stove disgusted by what I just saw—my appetite was gone. What the hell was I going to do now? My life was over, I should never have moved into her place, now I am stuck and have nowhere to go. I went back downstairs so I would not cause a scene and waited until I heard the front door close a few minutes later. I called my girl downstairs so we could talk. I told her that I saw everything and asked her if she wanted me to leave so she could have the girl. She began to cry. Shit! I did not expect that. She never cries. She admitted she was unsure of what she wanted. She did not know if she wanted another woman, if it was a phase, real, or if she still wanted me. How long would this nightmare last?

AFteR . . .

Why was I just crying? I'm a big girl, and I enjoyed the kiss that we just shared. Good thing he didn't see where her hands were or he would have flipped out. Was I crying because I was caught? No. Maybe I was crying because I was going to have to face the truth about myself. I tried to talk to him about what he just saw, but damn, where would I begin? Did I want her all the time or did I just enjoy the feelings I was having? I wasn't sure. I didn't tell him about my childhood, and that this wasn't the first time I had kissed a woman. I just said that I didn't know what I wanted because I wasn't ready to face reality. I knew my days were numbered, and I would have to eventually decide about my future. I wasn't ready for that level of commitment, attention, or test. I knew that I had to decide, so I approached him with a compromise. I asked him to give me his blessing to date the woman I desired. The woman I felt in my dreams. The woman I saw in my visions. I wanted to spend some time with her and figure out if my desires were true, and if not, I will be back to him fulltime. He blessed me with my request, which I didn't expect, because who in their right mind would agree to that? If the roles were reversed, his ass would have been on the street as soon as the basement door slammed shut. But I wasn't him, and he was still in love with me. So, he agreed, and I was able to spend time alone with her away from the house and prying eyes, in cities ranging from Philly to ATL.

SHARING SECRETS

I knew she was still seeing her "friend." Why did I allow this to continue? In my stupidity, I thought if I gave her time to process this relationship, she would come around, and I would get my girl back after she had had a chance to have the sexual experiences she wanted. But it did not end, she continued to lie to me at every opportunity so that she could see this woman. What was I doing that was so wrong? I needed someone to talk to and counseling wasn't helping. I needed to get her back to embarrass her like she was embarrassing me. I needed to vent and release my frustrations. My emotions were all over the place. Why was this happening to me? I planned to share our secret with her family so that she would suffer the way I was suffering now. Starting with telling her best friend about her double life. Why was I being punished? It was 7 p.m. and she still hadn't made it in from work.

Driving in the truck with her aunt, headed to the north side of the city, temptation came over me to casually mention what was happening at home. I told her all about the kiss I had witnessed and how I felt about it. But I asked that she didn't share the information with my girl. Asking that she don't share was a little reverse psychology, since I was secretly hoping that she would tell everyone in the family. I waited patiently for the fallout that I was hoping to see, but months passed, and I never heard a word about her relationship from her family. So, plan B was in full effect. I tracked down her best friend, and asked her out right if they were ever in a relationship. The response I received proved that her friend had no idea either. No one would tell her they knew. No one would shame her into returning to me. Six months remained on her allowable time to be with her girlfriend, and I didn't know what else to do to get her attention. Her birthday was approaching and thinking that I should do something drastic, I planned a surprise party for her. Gathering as many of her friends as I could find, we travelled to New Jersey for a surprise dinner. I had everyone in attendance: my family and hers. I was so nervous; I was about to do something crazy. Would she respond positively? I had no idea, but I was willing to put my pride on the line to save my relationship.

FINALLY

Today was a workout day. A day to hang with my girls at LA Fitness and to get kicked in the ass by the best spin instructor in Philly. I was hyped, more so than normally, because today my "dare" was coming true. Although we had hung out, we had never consummated our relationship, and I was certain I was ready for that step. I could hear my friends talking all around me about our upcoming New York trip. They were excited about the shows, the people, and the food. Our recently vegan friend kept talking about shopping. Girl, focus, I told myself when I missed a comment from my bestie. She was looking at me funny tonight. I didn't know what was up, but she kept asking me if I was ok. I knew she saw a difference tonight. I was not pushing or pedaling as hard as I normally did. I needed 7 p.m. to get here soon. My wish was about to come true. Off in the distance, I could hear the last song. My favorite jam, "Let's Get Married" by Run DMC and Jagged Edge. I kicked into high gear, singing along at a high, horrible pitch. I can't sing, y'all, but that's my jam. Finally, it was over, and I hopped off my bike, making my way into the locker room to shower. No time to dawdle; I had someone waiting for me and a debt to collect. I took the quickest shower in creation, threw on my tights with no undies for quick access, and drove across town. I was so excited, it was hard to focus on the GPS as I shot up the boulevard. Approaching the yellow light at Mascher Street, praying the red light didn't catch me because I was tired of giving the city my money. Slowing down through the restricted area at forty mph, I made it to Overbrook Park in record time. Sitting in the car, contemplating my next move. I was trying to get out of my head and follow my heart. I needed to make a decision; it was getting late, and I knew I needed to get home. Stepping out of the car would change my life forever. Although we had hung out, travelling and getting to know each other, stepping out of the car would change the course of my life forever. So, I sat there trying to decide what to do. Now that intimacy was on the table, and I was so close to her, I was terrified. My heart beat so loudly in my chest. I was frightened and intrigued. I opened the door and stepped out on faith. I slowly approached her front door. Each step felt like an eternity. I was scared shitless. I arrived at the top steps having second thoughts. I stepped back just as she opened the door to welcome me inside. Damn, she looked good. I bet she tastes as sweet. What the hell! Where did that come from? Those cat eyes had me. I walked toward her. Once inside, she wasted no time, pushing then pulling me upstairs toward her bedroom. Steam seemed to emanate between the two of us, and we hadn't even touched each other yet. She just looked at me, and then she asked me if I was sure. Before I could process her question, her lips were on mine. No, I wasn't ready, but damn, she felt good. Our tongues danced to a beat all their own. I don't remember being pushed back onto the bed and how my tights ended up on the floor. I was spread-eagled. She stood above me, looking down at me. She appeared to be much taller than her four foot, eleven inch frame. She looked into my eyes and asked me again if I was ready. I couldn't even think straight. I was at a loss for words. I mumbled a yes as she closed down on my clit. She ran her nails down my inner thighs, driving me crazy. Finally, I felt the tip of her tongue on my clit, instantly exciting me like no other. I came immediately, back-to-back orgasms rocked my soul. She refused to let up until I was completely saturated. More than an hour later she was still at it. How did all of this come from a woman? I begged to touch her, to please her as she was pleasing me. As I reached out to touch her, she took hold of my hands, placing my arms above my head. No touching at all for the remainder of the night. This is all about you, she said. She left me exhausted, saturated, and wanting to roll over and go to sleep. There would be no sleep for me; I needed to get my ass home to the other half.

AtL.

We planned this exciting getaway to ATL. The weekend would be an opportunity to bond with her and really see if the first sexual experience was a fluke. Everything was ready. I set the plan in motion to travel to South Carolina to visit family, but really, that was just a ploy. With the plan in place, airline tickets booked, and money in my pocket, we flew to Atlanta to have a weekend to remember.

My first trip to a strip club and it's the infamous Players Club. The Player's Club is a must-do whenever you're in the A. We went early enough to get good seats and not have to pay a cover charge. Two orders of wings and long island ice teas were on deck, and ass was everywhere. There was ass to the right of me and ass to the left of me. Then the skinniest stripper ever in creation came over to give me a lap dance. I wanted the thick chick I had been eyeing near the far side of the stage. She took off her thong; I was thinking damn girl, but it back on. I was amused, laughing at her while she danced in front of me. Less than ten minutes later, minus ten bucks, she left the area. I was in awe; someone was having sex in the booth upstairs in the corner. The VIP areas were beginning to set up and the late-night girls were showing up for work. The bartender was doing her job, since the first couple of drinks were good. Then in walked Shorty. A stocky, big-assed, brown-skinned mama. Although I was there with my boo thing, I couldn't take my eyes off this chick. She stayed over in the VIP area, talking to the fellas. Her walking around turned me on, and I started ignoring my lady. Every time she mentioned something to me, my focus constantly went back to the shorty with the big booty. Damn, Shorty was going to get me in trouble if I didn't focus. My boo wanted my attention—she desired my compliments, she had fire in her eyes from jealously. Ooh she wanted me bad. A couple of drinks later, it was time to be out. I didn't get another lap dance from the club, but my girl earned all those ones that were in my pocket.

She laid me down underneath her, staring into my eyes. She was ready, the excitement was evident. Slowly slipping me out of my jeans one leg at a time. She caressed me up and down my legs, causing goose bumps to appear, removing the rest of my clothing. I lay there in just my bra and panties, wild thoughts running through my head, pussy pulsating just from the sight of her hovering over me. She pulled off my panties first, then my bra, caressing me all over my body. The juices began to flow between my legs, her two hands felt like many, as she kissed me up and down both legs, blowing light caresses over my clit. I was on fire. She placed one, then the other breast in her mouth, paying extra attention to the areola. Fuck, I came. Not letting up just yet; she inserted her fingers inside of me, stroking softly at first, building the massive fire from within me. She laughed. She knew this game well and played it to a tee. Her motive was to show off and capture my heart in the process. She felt un-fucking-believable. The stroking increased, and I was coming apart. I begged her to stop. I couldn't catch my breath. How many orgasms could one person have? Another one was approaching quickly as all kinds of thoughts raced through my mind. I yelled out her name, begging and pleading for her to stop the torture. She wouldn't let up and I exploded against her fingers, trembling all over my body. I couldn't believe this was the best sex I had ever had. "Did a woman just do this to me?" She had and I was in love.

NOW WHAt?

I did this all wrong, I thought, as I sat in the restaurant waiting for her. I fucked her, and now I'm demanding she date me. WTF! Or better yet, she fucked me—I was just a willing participant. She approached the table and sat across from me. She was my first adult relationship, so I had a lot of questions about gender roles, masculine vs feminine women, and everything in between. I wanted to know who paid for dinner—she, me or both. She already opened car doors for me and walked on the street side when we were out and about, which I loved. Shit, I didn't want to be the first one hit by a car, lol. She answered my questions with no hesitation, but was shocked when I told her I wanted more than what we had shared that one night in ATL. We agreed to meet the following week in Manayunk for dinner. We walked along the historic neighborhood on Main Street, holding hands. I subconsciously let go of her hand every time I saw someone I thought I knew, if people stared too hard, or if I just felt self-conscious. I asked for an opportunity to get to know her, but I was not ready. I wasn't ready to confess to my family and friends that I was in love with a woman. I wasn't ready to explain this to my kids, but I pretended in that moment to be. Holding hands and strolling along the walking trails, window-shopping, and talking. We talked about everything and anything, just getting to know each other more. My focus was on learning as much as I could about her likes, dislikes, and hobbies. The bedroom antics only last for so long; I was determined to capture her mind as well as she did my body. I needed to work on my acceptance of myself first. Travelling always helped me focus and Egypt was the place to start.

Riding to JFK to catch a fourteen-hour flight to Egypt was frightening. I asked him to drive me there to meet up with her. This is when I knew I had completely lost my mind. What the hell was I thinking, whisking away with her to spend nine days in Egypt? He didn't ask me who I was going with or anything else. I made up some story, but I didn't want to be honest, and I didn't realize I should have just confessed. I stood in line waiting for her to appear, and I kept looking over my shoulders because I could feel someone staring at me. I could feel him lurking in the shadows at one of the entrances. I kept looking around and never saw him, but I knew he was watching me. We landed in Egypt and met up with the tour guide. First stop after customs was the hotel in Cairo. I unpacked my bag to find two bottles of champagne and a note that read, Enjoy your time with your soul mate. I will be gone when you return. And just like that, he left me. I could never choose between the two of them because he was comfort, but she was home. He made the decision for me. I will be forever grateful to him for the first push. Now I'm running. There's a whole world out there for us to explore, and I'm holding on tight to her as we journey through this thing called life as one.